T0197343

Baby Name Inspiration

Baby Names You Love and Can Pronounce

Rasheema Owens

Trafford rev. 05/30/2015

 www.trafford.com

North America & international
toll-free: 1 888 232 4444 (USA & Canada)
fax: 812 355 4082

CONTENTS

December 26, 2008

ACKNOWLEDGEMENTS

First, I would like to thank my <u>Lord and Savior Jesus Christ</u> for birthing this vision of writing my own name book. I've always enjoyed naming people's children. Every time I came across a unique name, I wrote it down as a hobby, not thinking anything special about it. I just wanted to remember the name. This baby name book has been inspired from decades ago when I was a student in middle school. That is why I called it BABY NAME INSPIRATION! Thank you Lord for allowing this name book to become a reality and an accomplishment.

Last, I would like to thank everyone else who have given their names and ideas to assist me in my inspiration. Furthermore, I really thank my readers who purchased this baby name book, and I pray it will be a blessing to you, whether you are 1) thinking about a child, 2) already pregnant, 3) about to deliver, 4) want to name someone in your family, or 5) just plain curious to see what names are out there. You shall be enlightened by scripture, words of encouragement, songs, poems, and anything else that inspired you while you read. Remember, every name you see was inspired by someone or something.

FOREWARD

On a side note, let me know if you know someone with a name in this book or you heard of that particular name, or if you come across a name that inspired you, then please feel free to contact me at:

Rasheema M. Owens, FL
(561) 414-0801

I would love to hear from you, about what inspired you the most or the least, or just wanted to contact me to make a name addition. Thank you very much.

Please Note: **It's purposely not in any particular alphabetical order. Other spellings of the same name are indented.**

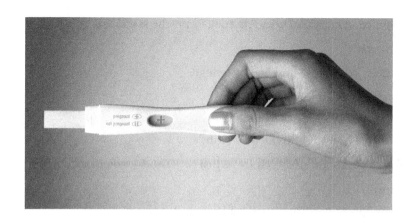

INSPIRED BY SCRIPTURE
MATTHEW 7:7

A—*Ask* & You shall receive.

Arianna

Alehandra & Alehandria (inspired by twins)

Alexandria & Alexandre (inspired by twins)

Audreana

Amari

Ameran & Amberlyn (inspired by twins on 12/31/08)
 Amerin, Ameryn, Ameren
 Amberlyne, Amberline, Amberlen

Armyas & Camias (inspired by twins)

Azhiya & Aniyah (inspired by twins)
 Azaiah, Aazaiah, Azayiah, Azayah
 Anaiyah, Anyiah, Anhiya, Aaniya

Ameree, Amery, Amerie, Amarie (all pr. the same)

Arniece

Arnessa & Vanessa (inspired by twins)

Avien & Aiden (inspired by twins)
　　　Adan, Aden

Anansey & Ayansi (inspired by twins)

Aram & Abram (inspired by twins)

Aunica

Armonte & Armand (inspired by twins)

Alaska, Ailaska

Alasqua, Alaskwa, Ailaskwa (all pr. the same)

Ari, Aari

Amara (pr. Am mer ah or Ah mar rah,)

Aratani & Altani (inspired by twins)

Aria, Arrea, Areea, Areeya' (all pr. R E A)

Airea, Ariye, Ariay, (all pr. Air e a)

Aliciana, Aliseana, Eliseana (all pr. the same)

Alauna & Alaun (inspired by twins)
　　　Alonah, Alona

Aquarian, Aquarien

Acarian & Anedian (pr. A ney dee an)
　　　Akarian, Akarean, Akarian, Acarien, Acarean, Akareane
　　　(inspired by Kerry & Ren)

Ataviana Moesa (pr. Mo e sa) (inspired by Cousin Lisa & first and middle name)

Adien & Avien (inspired by twins)
　　　Adien, Adean, Adian, Adein (pr. A D N)
　　　Avien, Avean, Avian, Aveiin (pr. A V N)

Annea (pr. A knee yah)
    Anneya, Aneyia, Aneia, Anneah, Aneea, Aaneyah

Adriel

Ambrien, Ambrean

Aven & Neva (inspired by twins, names in reciprocal order)

Asher, Acher (means blessed)

Adar & Kedar (inspired by twins)

Addam

Aida (pr. Ida)

Alexah & Alexin (inspired by twins)

Aquina & Aquila (inspired by twins)
    Aquinnah & Aquillah

Aschka & Ascham (pr. Ash kim, inspired by twins, 10/6/12)

Achan (inspired by Joshua 7:1, pr. A kin or Ah khan)

Adonijah (pr. A don ee jah, inspired by II Samuel 3:2)

Achish (pr. A kish, inspired by I Samuel 21:10)

Arioch (inspired by Daniel 2:24, contributed 9/22/10)

Akimat (contributed by Hakim, Tamika spelled backwards)

Ameehsar (pr. Amee shar), this is my daughter's name, inspired by Rasheema, mommy's name, spelled backwards

Avatar, Avahtar, Avathar, Aavatar (all pr. the same)

Amik, Imik, Emik (all pr. A meek or Ah meek)

Azzoya (inspired by Patrice's daughter's name, 6/20/12)

Aryk (pr. Eric inspired by Kyra spelled backwards (7/9/12)

Ayar & Raya (inspired by twins, reciprocal spellings)

Ambrielle

Armee & Navee (pr. Army & Navy, inspired by twins)

Arben & Nebra (inspired by reciprocal twin names)

Alten & Alven (inspired by twins) other spellings are Altan & Alvan

Amren (inspired by Biblical name Amram in Exodus 6:20)

Arrow & Arrou (pr. A ru), inspired by twins, 12/30/13

Asariel (pr. A zar ree el) Jerubi (inspired by first & middle name, 1/15/14

Ayotal (inspired by Latoya spelled backwards)

Ameia (pr. Ah me ya) (inspired by my son giving his sister, Ameehsar, a nickname, 11/12/13 – Other spellings are Ameea, Ameya, Amea, Ahmeah, Ameeya (all pr. the same)

Asante Sana & Etnasa Anas (inspired by reciprocal twins, first & middle names)

Aerinehe (pr. Ah ren neh he) & Aeroniche (pr. Aaron ne che) (inspired by twins)

Aliehs (pr. Aleish) (inspired by Sheila spelled backwards)

Azare (pr. A zair re), Azere (pr. A zeer re), Azire (pr. A zy re), Azore (pr. A zore re), & Azure (pr. A zur re) (all pr. differently with all vowels)

Almasi Monefa (inspired by my son's dental receptionist name, Almasi means diamond or pertaining to diamond & Monefa means the lucky one

Adaj (inspired by Jada spelled backwards) & Aoj (pr. Ahjh) inspired by twins

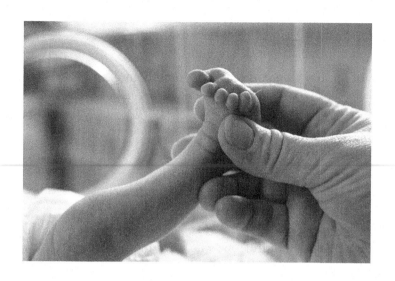

INSPIRED BY ENCOURAGEMENT

B—*Be* not concerned with the devil's devices.

Brenton & Branden (inspired by twins)

Brooklin, Brookllyn, Brookelyn (all pr. the same)

Benzi

Badieh (pr. Ba di ya) & Zekiah (inspired by twins)

Brequan

Boniquea

Breunice, Breaniece

Beige, Baige

Belgy (contributed by Ebony, 9/17/10)

Bryceton (contributed by Ebony, 9/17/10)

Braden (contributed by Ebony, 9/17/10)

Briony (contributed 10/6/12)

Balendin (means strong or brave in Latin)

Bayani (pr. bay ah nee, means hero in Philipino)

Brant

Benecia

Bellanca

Bailynn

Bency (means nice girl in Hindu)

Bonamy (means good friend in French)

Braeton (means beautiful, one who loves another)

Braylen

Bryce (means swift or quick-moving in Celtic)

Brielle Trevin & Briella Trevisa (inspired by girl & boy twins, Brielle means exalted goddess in French, also Briella Trevisa are names of Boynton Beach community homes, 1/18/14

Breillan Palais (pr. Palace) inspired by first & middle name

Brillan & Dillan (inspired by first & middle name)

Brocklyn, Brooklyn, & Brocklye (pr. Broccoli) inspired by triplets, Other spellings are Brockelyn, Brookelyn , & Brockelyee

Briley (means steady or strong in Scottish)

Brogan (means sturdy or strong)

Brityn & Brilye (inspired by twins)

Bynah

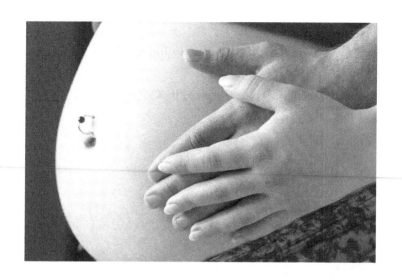

INSPIRED BY SCRIPTURE
MATTHEW 11:28

C—*Come* unto me all ye heavy laden &
I will give you rest.

Charvessa (pr. Sh)

Chelisa (pr. Sh)

Caleb (pr. K, means king or leader)

Canden (pr. K)

Chemarcus (pr. Sh) & Chemari (pr. Sh) (inspired by twins)

Clence & Clance (inspired by Clarence)

Clinton & Clandon (inspired by twins)

Carmiah

Chenaya (pr. Sh)

Charmeila (pr. K or Sh)

Chandia (pr. Shon dee ah) & Chandeya (pr. Shon day ah) (inspired by twins)

Corheem, Careem, Coreem (inspired by Corey & Raheem)

Corey, Coree, Corree

Charen (pr. K)

Chandey (pr. Sh)

Chantilee (pr. Sh)

Chanta (pr. Sh)

Chakyra (pr. Sh)

Carmontas

Chellsey (pr. Ch) & Shellsei (inspired by twins)
    Chellsea, Shellcee

Chawncey (pr. Ch or Sh)

Carlos

Carnetta & Carnitta (inspired by twins)

Carneissa & Charneysa (pr. Sh) (inspired by twins)

Chandra Kenicia (pr. Ken e sha)

Chandrea (pr. Sh) & Chaundera (pr. Shon day ra) (inspired by twins)
    Chendaira

Chanelli (pr. Sh)

Coral, Corale, Korell (all pr. the same)

Chara (pr. K or Sh) (inspired by scripture I Corinthians 1:7 means joy, cheerfulness, delight)

Cheshia, Chisha (pr. Keisha)

Cheisa (pr. Keisa)

Cheilal (pr. Kee i lol)

Charity

Chekanna (pr. Sh) & Chekani (pr. She khon knee)

Charlette & Charla

Charette

Cheranne (pr. She rawn), Sherawne (girl), Cheraun (boy), Cheron

Cheniina (pr. She nina) & Chaneema (pr. Sh)

Cabrum & Camden (inspired by twins)

Cabra, Caybra, Kabra, Kaybra (all pr. the same)

Chebony, Cheveny, Chevanny, Chevanni, Shevenni (all pr. the same)

Chiy, Chai (pr. Khi)

Chaunessi (pr. Shawn ness ee)

Chaughney, Chaunay (pr. Shawn neigh)

Chequanda, Chequonda (pr. Sh)

Canyon

Cynthea

Cindee, Syndy

Ceeja, Cejaa (pr. C J)

Cayen, Kayen (pr. K N)

Cana Akoya (inspired by first and middle name)

Crystal

Canalle (pr. Canal)

Coren, Coryn, Coreyn (all pr. the same)

Cassidy

Chaaz, Chaz, Chazz (contributed 8/31/09, all pr. the same)

Caden (pr. K, contributed 12/30/09)

Chrisena, Crisena, Chrissenya, Chriseyna (all pr. the same)

Chantilee

Chashar (pr. Kah-shar) inspired by Ecclesiastes 11:6 means to prosper, successful, right, proper

Chaminee, Chamenaa (pr. Sha men a, 1/19/11)

Chimberly & Chandler (inspired by boy/girl twins)

Canya & Cenya (both pr. with S, inspired by twins)

Cressie & Cassie (inspired by twins)

Craigton, contributed 3/13/15

Chenani (inspired by Nehemiah 9:4, contributed 4/20/14)

Chayah (pr. K ya, inspired by Habakkuh 2:5, means "shall live, flourish, be preserved)

Camron Jatore (inspired by first & middle name, Cameron & Jatara, 2/17/14)

Cadell & Madell (inspired by twins)

INSPIRED BY SCRIPTURE
MATTHEW 7:12

D—*Do* unto others as you would have them
do unto you.

Deirdre

Desiree

Daira & Daisha (inspired by twins)

Daxious, Dextias, & Decias (inspired by triplets)

Dexter & Dexmond (inspired by twins)

Dehira

Dimarco-lamar, Dimarco Larmar

Derrica & Derric (inspired by twins, contributed Aug. 2010, means a road, course, ways, or mode of action from Proverbs 3:5-6)
Darec, Derek, Darick, Darik, Darec, Dareck

Darique, Dareek, Dareeke, Daricke, Dereek, Derique, Dariiq (all pr. the same)

Dekarai (means happiness in Africa)

Deneysia, D'Naja, D'Naija (pr. Den neigh jsha)

Decota & Desota (inspired by twins, other pr. are Dekota, Decoata, Desoata, Dasota)

Dextarra, D'Xstara, Dxstara, Dexstarra (all pr. the same)

Dontravius, Dontrevious, Dontrevius, Dontravies, Dontrayvias (all pr. the same)

Dontray, Dontrey, Dontre, Dantre (all pr. the same)

DeNashua

Devina, Daveena (inspired by Deville & Medina)

Denver Zeroyce (inspired by first & middle name, contributed by Walter 7/20/14)

Diamond

Dellon & Dillon (inspired by twins)

D'hanen, D'hana, & D'haka (written 07/22/09) (inspired by triplets)
D'hennin, D'hannen

Dareyon & Daveion (inspired by twins)
Dariyon, Dareun
Davion, Daveon

Denisa (inspired by Dennis & Lisa or Daniel & Lisa)
Daneisa, Danisa

Dezinati, Dezinatty

Demelan (inspired by Dexter & Melanie, 05/2010)

Darielle (pr. Dare ee l) & Danielle (inspired by twins, contributed 10/21/10)

Drayce, Dreyce, Drace (all pr. the same, contributed 6/06/11)

David & Davod (inspired by twins, 12/29/10)
  Da'Ved, Dayvid, Dayved (all pr. David)

  Davade, Davaid, Davaad (all pr. Da'Vod)

Daniel & Danuel (pr. Da nool or Dan u el, inspired by twins 6/22/11)

Dexstinee, Dexstiny (inspired by Dexter, 6/20/12)

Darnelle & Darshelle (inspired by twins, 6/25/14)

Dael, Diel, & Duel (inspired by triplets)

Diel Jerue (inspired by names on tractor trailers, first & middle name, contributed 5/17/14)

Dunamis (pr. Doo nam is, inspired by Acts 4:33, means energy, power, might, great force, great ability & strength, 4/21/14)

Deasa (inspired by radio commercial, 4/30/14)

Damaris, Damauro, & Damar (inspired by triplets, 12/9/13)

Dalland (pr. Day land, all pr. the same, Daeland, Daelane, Dalen, Daelin)

Darrington & Carrington (inspired by twins)

Diantay (contributed 4/28/12, other pr. Dyantae, Diante, Dyante, Dyantay, Dyanta')

INSPIRED BY SCRIPTURE
PSALMS 150:6

E—Let *everything* that has breath,
praise the Lord.

Ezekiel Tary (inspired by first and last name)

Ezavier Tony (inspired by first and last name)

Ezraiel Terel (inspired by first and last name)
(Ezekiel, Ezavier, Ezraiel are inspired by triplets or three brothers.)

Ezaiah (pr. Ez)

Ebonica (pr. Eb on ee ka, inspired by best friend, Ebony's name)

Evian & Ebiann (inspired by twins)

Exzabia & Exzaria (inspired by twins)

Eyoni

Edan (inspired by Ebony & Daniel)

Eirene (pr. eye ray nay) (inspired by Luke 1:79, means peace, comes from Irene)

Echad, Achad (inspired by scripture Deuteronomy 6:4, means one or unity)

Echan, Achan

Elbin (contributed by Ebony)

Estafany (contributed by Ebony) & Estifanny (inspired by twins)

E'Zaria, Azaria (contributed by Ebony)

Ellington (contributed by Ebony)

Eoj (inspired by Joe spelled backwards, 6/25/11, pr. E - oj)

Ehsia (pr. Ah c ah or pr. E c ah, written Aishe – pr. Iesha, spelled backwards, 6/22/11)

Ericaria

Enjoya & Enjara (inspired by twins)

Ellenys (pr. El len nis, inspired by Synelle spelled backwards, 10/28/12)

Estani, Estiani, Estefani, & Esani (inspired by quadruplets)

Ethan & Eastan (inspired by twins)

Eweandi (can be pronounced U wan dee or creatively pr. (You and I) & inspired by Eweami (pr. You and my – a lady I met on a condo tour)

INSPIRED BY SCRIPTURE
HEBREWS 11:1 & PHILIPPIANS 3:13

F—*Faith* is the substance of things hoped for &
Forget those things which are behind.

Fraan (pr. Fron)

Frantz (contributed by Ebony, 7/24/09)

Faliiq, Falique

Felipe (contributed by Ebony, 7/24/09)

Fatima (contributed by Ebony, 9/17/10)

Faye (contributed by Ebony, 9/17/10)

Fabien & Felecian (inspired by twins, 10/6/12)

Facynthia

Fidel (means faithful in Spanish, from late Latin name Fidelis, contributed 10/6/12)

Farid (pr. Fa reed)

Farren (pr. Fare n) & Factor (inspired by twins)

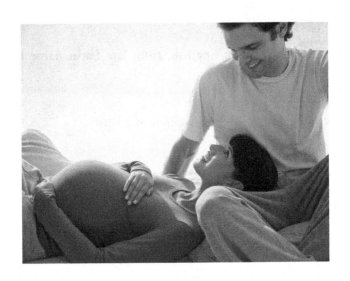

INSPIRED BY SCRIPTURE
LUKE 6:38

G—*Give* and it shall be given unto you, pressed down, shaken together, and running over.

Genossi, Janossi (pr. Gen no see, inspired by Mom)

Gervais (inspired by Suelain May, author of Names to Grow On, 2007)

Gunthar & Guntharius (inspired by Suelain May, author of Names to Grow On, 2007)

Gynell (inspired by Suelain May, author of Names to Grow On, 2007)

Garron (contributed 10/6/12)

Gable

Galvin

Gevira

Galana

Galia

Gabir

Gaza

Gamil (pr. ga meal or ja meal)

Galit (pr. ga leet or ja leet)

Ghalib (means "conqueror" in Arabic)

Galexy

Glacier

Glava

INSPIRED BY SCRIPTURE
I SAMUEL 16:7 & PROVERBS 3:9

H—The Lord looks at the *heart* & *Honor* the
Lord with your possessions and
your firstfruit of all your increase.

Hadar (inspired by Psalms 8:5 means honor)

Harmony (contributed by Ebony, 9/17/10)

Hakim (means in Arabic, wise one 6/09/11)

Hamir & Harim (inspired by twins, 3/1/12)

Halvard (contributed 10/6/12)

Halim (pr. Ha leem)

Hanif (pr. Ha neef)

Hanley

Handira & Handria (inspired by twins)

Hanita

Hadara & Hadia (inspired by twins)

Hovan (means "God is gracious", Short form of Armenian Hovhannes)

Henrique (means "home-ruler" in Portuguese, form of Latin Henricus)

Herrick

Hairam (inspired by Mariah spelled backwards – pr. Hi rum) 11/27/14

Hawyan (pr. Hawaiian)

INSPIRED BY SCRIPTURE
ST. JOHN 14:6 & PHILIPPIANS 4:13

I—*I* am the way, the truth, and the life &
I can do all things through Christ.

Irian

Ienya

Izavier

Imani (means faith) & Imari (inspired by twins)

Iysia & Aysia (pr. Asia) (inspired by twins)

Isah & Isan (a German name, inspired by Lareina Rule, author of
Name Your Baby, 1986, means Iron – willed one)

Ishmar (contributed by Ebony, 7-24-09) & Keshmar (inspired by
twins, contributed by church friend's son)

Ishmael (inspired by Genesis 16:16)

Idalia (contributed by Ebony) & Idalis (inspired by twins)

Iliana (contributed by Ebony, 9/17/10)

Imasia, Emesia, Imasya, Amaisia, Imisia, Imisia, Amisieh (all pr. the same Ah ma c ah, 6/22/11)

Ivone (pr. Yvonne)

Izhar & Rahzi (inspired by reciprocal twins, Exodus 6:18)

Islan & Ailan (pr. Island)

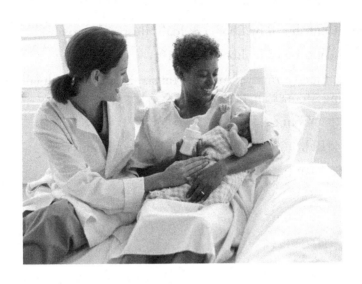

INSPIRED BY SONG

J—*Joy* to the world the Lord has come.

Jenavanni

Jacob Ezra (inspired by first and last name)

Joshua

Jason

Jemarcus & Jemari (inspired by twins)

Jemarria & Jemarquin (inspired by twins)

Janeca (pr. John ik a)

Jakyri, Jhakyri (pr. Ja ki ree)

Josten & Justen (inspired by twins)

Jocelyn & Jacquelyn (inspired by twins)

Jhakeri (pr. Ja care ee) & Jachery (Jack er ree) (inspired by twins)

Jerhonda

Jaylur

Jakhaya, Jekhaya

Joreiah (pr. Jo ri ah) & Jharieh (pr. Jar ee ah) (inspired by twins)

Jaliik (pr. Ja leek)

Jalecia, Jaleesia

Jalexia & Janicea (inspired by twins)

Jorrah & Zarrah (inspired by twins)

Jhakisea (pr. Ja kee see ah) (inspired by Cousins Jackie & Keisha)
& Jhakesa (inspired by twins)

Jabe

Jheraa (pr. Jer rah) & Jheray (pr. Jer ray) (inspired by twins)

Jyaile (pr. Jhi yale)

Jimaar & Jebarree (inspired by twins)
    Jebare, Jabare, Jebari (means brave in African)

Jameesa, Jamisa

Jhaiem (pr. Jhi eem) & Zieem (inspired by twins)

Janarious & Janarice (comes from January & Maurice, inspired by
twins)
    Januareus, Januarias, Janareus, Janarias

Jeremiah

Jaycee & Jayce (inspired by twins)

Jewan, Jewon, Jewaan, Juwan (inspired by my son's middle name,
and Jenny & Juan)

Jerrica & Jericho (inspired by twins)
    Jericha, Jerricha
    Jerricho, Jerrico

Jazreen, Jazreann, & Jazriana (inspired by triplets)
    Jazriann
    Jazrean

Jeshurun (means upright one, Proverbs 3:6, Deuteronomy 3:5, 33:15, Isaiah 44:2),

      Jeshuran, Jeshuren, Jeshuraan, Jeshuron

Jalon (pr. Jah lawn) & Jalen (pr. Jah lynn or Jay lynn) (inspired by twins, boy & girl, 9/22/10)

Jobert

Juraan

Jetauni, Jataani

Jaterri & Jaterra (inspired by twins)

Jonelli

Jobard

Jbard, Jebard

Jacom, Jakum

Jwadaja, Jewadaja

Jakaa, Jacaa, Jakay, J'Kay (pr. J K)

Jayka, Jaca

Jaisonna, Jasahna

Jasonica (inspired by Jason & Monica)

Jusennia & Jasaanea (inspired by twins)

Jacayla

Jessica

Jimenee, Jimenie

Janiza & Juliza (inspired by twins)

Jyias, Jias, Jaias (all pr. the same)

Jaza, Jaiza, Jayza (all pr. the same)

Jewel

Jysteria (inspired by Cousin Stephanie)

Jamiyeh (pr. Ja my ah) & Jameela

Jamer (pr. Ja mayor or Ja mirror)

Jaquez, Jacques (pr. Ja qwezz, 10/1/10)

Jenrikesha

Jared

Journey (contributed 7/30/12)

Javid & Javod (inspired by twins, 12/29/10)
    Javaid, Javade (both pr. like David)
    Javod, Javaad (pr. like Da'Vod)

Jasiel (inspired by Joshua, 7/5/14)

Jester & Jasper (inspired by twins)

Jamin (inspired by scripture Exodus 6:15)

Jaicis (pr. Jay Isis)

Jeshante (contributed 4/28/12)

JayNyla Sadore (inspired by first & middle name, other pr. J'Nyla or Janyla)

Jeiada (pr. Je ida) inspired by scripture Jeremiah 29:26, priest name Jehoiada

Jerdan & Jordan (inspired by twins)

Jazer (inspired by 1 Chronicles 26:31, 6/26/11)

Jerijah (inspired by 1 Chronicles 26:31, 6/26/11)

INSPIRED BY SCRIPTURE
I KINGS 6:12

K—*Keep* my commandents.

Kelicia Tanique (inspired by first and middle name)

KeeIdah (pr. Ke ida) & KeeIlah (pr. Ke i la) (inspired by twins)

Kenton

Keshanee

Kemari, Kimaree

Korea, Coreya (contributed 7/27/10)

Kenneth & Kennedy (inspired by twins)

Kansas

Kimberlyn, Kimberlin, Kembirlyn (all pr. the same)

Kemiah, (pr. Ka my ah)

Kaylen

Kyri & Kyra (inspired by twins)

Kyle, Caial (pr. the same)

Khanda (pr. Konda, inspired by Karen & Shonda)

Kaaza (contributed by friend Tia's daughter's name)

Kylee

Kelcey

Kelliyn

Kinshay

Kasera, Kasarah, Kesara, Kesarra, Caserah (all pr. the same)

Kaveus, Kavius, Kavias, Caveus, Cavius (all pr. the same)

Kayah (pr. Kay ya) & Khiya (pr. Khi) (inspired by twins)

Kester

Khiy, Khai (pr. K + hi)

Ketre, Ketrea, Ketree (all pr. the same)

Kinyna (pr. Kenya) Jazmin (inspired by first and middle name)

Kayen, Cayen (pr. K N)

Kayem, Kaym, Cayem, Caym (pr. K M)

Koyale & Royale (inspired by twins, girl and boy)

Keneveni (pr. Ken nev ven knee) & Keveny (pr. Kevin knee) (inspired
by twins)
     Keveni, Keviney

Kaleciana, Kalesciana (pr. K lease see ah na)

Ketundra, Keitundra, Keitondra, Keitaundra
(all pr. the same, inspired by Keith & Shawndra)

Keitreana, Ketreaina, Keitreaina, Keitreanna, Ketriana (all pr. the
same)

Kemyla & Kesaiya (inspired by twins)
     Kesiiah, Kesiyah, Kesaya

Kayden Acarien (inspired by first and middle name)
    Caiden (contributed by co-worker Robyn's son's name)

Kiireah (pr. Ki air e uh) & Kimareah (inspired by twins, 7/27/10)
    Kamureah, Kimarrea

Keedar, Kiydar, Keydar, Qidar (all pr. the same)

Kandice

Karec, Kerec, Kerek, Karac, Karik, Kareck, Kerick, Karick (all pr. the same)

Kareah (inspired by Jeremiah 42:1, 7/27/10)

Ketai (pr. Kee tie)

Katarian, Ketariun, Ketarien, Katarean (all pr. the same)

Kimaka Mikayla (inspired by first & middle name 1/15/2011)

Klarey, Klaree, Klarry (all pr. the same)

Kashim & Kashib (inspired by twins, the I is pr. e)

Kashim & Mishak (inspired by twins, reciprocal spellings)

Kasheb Kurtne (inspired by first & middle)

Kahim 3/1/12

Kian (pr. Key n, inspired by Kia & Ian)

Kandler

Keesheaay (contributed 10/6/12, pr. Keesh she a)

Kenton

Khanya (pr. Con ya) & Khenya (inspired by twins)

Keegan & Kaagan (inspired by twins, 12/17/13)

Keenan & Kaanan (inspired by twins, 12/17/13)

Kestaria (contributed 11/5/14)

Karati (pr. Karate) & Kareta (pr. Kar ee ta or K reta) (inspired by twins)

INSPIRED BY SCRIPTURE
I JOHN 4: 8, 16

L—God is *love.*

Larin (written 10-26-08, inspired by Pastor Lance & Sis. Marilane)

Lacorey, Lucorey

Lawrenz, Larenz

Lorence

Lasharveay (pr. La shar vee aa)

Latieja (pr. La tee asia or La tee jah)

Lambert

Latifya (pr. La tif ee ah)

Lakevia

Lake

LaQuinton Zh'vae (contributed by my cousin's son's first and middle name)

Lakasia (pr. La kay jha) Brinique (inspired by my cousin's daughter's first and middle name)

Lutron (inspired by Matthew 20:28, means ransom—a release from slavery or captivity, the price paid cancelling our debt.)

Lamad (pr. La mahd, means teaches, to instruct, train, teach, learn, goad, Isaiah 48:17)

Londen & Lynden (inspired by twins, 6/06/11)

    Londin & Lyndin

Liruq, Liruc (pr. Lee rook, inspired by Willie & Faruq, contributed 6/22/11)

Lamaj (inspired by Jamal spelled backwards, 7/4/12)

Lianyce (pr. Lee un niece), contributed 7/5/14

Leahcar (pr. Lee car) inspired by Rachael spelled backwards

Lais & Luis (inspired by twins)

INSPIRED BY WORDS OF ENCOURAGEMENT

M—*May* the Lord watch between me and thee.

Monica

Mekayla & Meshayla (inspired by twins)

Merari (pr. Me rare e) (inspired by the Bible—The Living Translation Exodus 6:16, 19)

Mahli

Mahlik (pr. Ma leek) & Maleki (pr. Mal i khi) (inspired by twins)

Matthew

Michigan & Michiga (inspired by twins)

Madecyn (pr. Ma den sin)

Markarria, Markary, & Markarius (inspired by triplets)
> Marquaria
> Marquarias, Markarious
> Marquary, Markarry, Markarey

Marqueyla (pr. Mar key la)

Marcus Alexander (inspired by first and middle name)

Maleah, Maleea, Maleeya (all pr. the same)

Maryssa (pr. Mae rissa) Jalaan (pr. Ja lon)
(contributed by my cousin's daughter's first & middle name)

Melan, Melaan, Melaon, Melawn, Melaun (all pr. the same, inspired by Melanie, 05/2010)

Michael & Micahel (pr. Ma kay uhl, inspired by twins)

Mayim (pr. My eem, means waters, Isaiah 43:2, contributed 10/23/10)

Micaela (pr. Mic a ail la) Jasmina (inspired by first & middle name, contributed by Denise's daughter's name, 12/28/10)

Mykaar (contributed by Hakim &Rasheema 6/22/11

MiNerva (contributed by Hakim, Hakim's grandmother's middle name, 6/22/11)

Miksha (pr. Meek sha, contributed by Hakim 6/22/11, inspired by Tamika & Iesha)

Mishud & Mishun (inspired by twins, 6/22/11)

Mizahria (contributed 7/3/11)

Makaya & Makeya (inspired by twins, 7/29/11))
    Macaia, Mecaia, Mekaia & Maceia, Maceya, Maqeia, Maqueya

Mizhara, Mizharvia, Mizharia (inspired by triplets)
        Mezhara, Mezharvea, Mezharea

Mishara, Misharvia, Misharia (inspired by triplets, 10/5/12)

Mizanee, Mezani, Mezhani (all pr. the same)

Machir & Machira (inspired by scripture Genesis 50:23, Manasseh's only son) pr.: the Ch is pr. with a K, boy & girl twins

Madellan, Magellan, & Medallion (inspired by triplets)

INSPIRED BY SONG BY MARVIN SAPP

N—*Never* would have made it without you.

Nekira TiJae (inspired by first and middle name)

Novartis Chavawn inspired by first and middle name)

Nechunta (pr. Na shon ta) & Nichenta (pr. Nhi shen ta)

Nirayeh (pr. Na rye ya) and Zuriyah (pr. Za rye ya)
 Neriya, Narieya

Nadeja (pr. Na dee jsha) & Nadaja (pr. Na day sha) (inspired by twins)
 Naideja, Nideja, Nideeja, Nidaaja (all pr. Na day sha)

Nyasia, Naiaja (pr. Nhi a jsha) (inspired by twins)

Naema (pr. Nhi ee ma) & Naomi (inspired by twins)

Naeem (means benevolent in Africa)

Nehemiah, Nejemiah

Nekiyah (pr. Na khi yah) & Nezyiah (pr. Na zhi yah) (inspired by twins)

Nekhiya, Nekhaya, Nakhaya Nazhiya, Nezhaya, Neziya

Nakham (pr. Na kim) & Nachem (pr. Na chim) (inspired by twins)

Nevaeh (pr. Na veigh like sleigh, inspired by my cousin's daughter's middle name, heaven spelled backwards)

Navien & Dinabian (pr. Di nay bee in, inspired by twins, 9/11/10)

Nelej (inspired by Jalen spelled backwards, 7/4/12)

Nichae (pr. Ni shay, inspired by mother-in-law oldest daughter's middle name, 9/29/12)

Noret (pr. No ray or the t is silent, inspired by Teron spelled backwards – one of my student's name, contributed 12/18/13)

Norie & Noriece (inspired by twins)

Nostalgia & Natalya (inspired by twins)

Nedrika & Akirden (inspired by reciprocal twins names spelled backwards) Nedrika is a person I met at CarMax, service operator.

Nyla & Nyrou (inspired by twins) means strength and power. Both names backwards are Alyn Uoryn (pr. your rye an)

INSPIRED BY SCRIPTURE
I CHRONICLES 16:8

O—*Oh,* give thanks unto the Lord.

Ojhona (pr. O john na)

Orecia (pr. O reese see ah)

Obaria Baray (inspired President Barak Obama, 2009)

Olena (means light in Russia, inspired by Lareina Rule, author of Name Your Baby, 1986)

Ozora (means strength of the Lord in Hebrew, inspired by Lareina Rule, author of Name Your Baby, 1986)

Olan, Olen (contributed 9/22/10)

Olaine (contributed 9/22/10)

Ozaria & Ozar (inspired by twins, contributed 9/22/10)

Onez

Odil

Orell & Oriel (inspired by twins)

Oriana

Onessa

Osamu (means "discipline, study" in Japanese)

Osher (means "happiness" in Hebrew)

Orlanda

Orita

Orchesis

Orchid

Olivia & Olive (inspired by twins)

INSPIRED BY SCRIPTURE
JAMES 5:16

P—The effectual fervent *prayer* of
a righteous man availeth much.

Prenton & Pranden (inspired by twins)

Phenix

Phoenicia & Phenicia (inspired by twins)
     Phonencia (inspired by Acts 21:1-2)

Patara

Parker

Peyton, Payton

Parrhesia (pr. par rhay see ah) (inspired by Acts 4:31 means boldness, contributed 7-24-09, not a human quality but a result of being filled with the Holy Spirit, Word Wealth from Spirit-Filled Life Bible p. 1632, copyright 1991)

Palis (contributed 8/31/09)

Paige, Peige

Peale (pr. Peel) & Paile (pr. Pail) (inspired by twins)

Pepper

Pernell & Parnell (inspired by twins)

Paley & Parry (inspired by twins)

Packard

Payjah

Panyin

Pagnier (pr. Pahn yay) & Piaget (inspired by twins 10/29/12)

Pavi (contributed 10/6/12)

INSPIRED BY POEM

𝒬—Don't *Quit.*

Quenton Zhavei (pr. Za vay), Quenci Harvii (pr. Har vay), Qaton (pr. Ka ten) Jharvi (pr. Jar vay) (inspired by triplets' first and middle names)
> Quentin
> Quinci
> Caton, Qatin (pr. Ka ten)

Qeyon (pr. Key on) Carlos, Quelon (pr. Kwe on) Quelos (pr. Kwe los), Quelon (pr. Key lon) Juelos (pr. Hway los), and Qayon (pr. Kay on) Calos (pr. Kay los)
> (inspired by quadruplets' first and last names)

Quenshai (pr. Kwhen shay)

Qutrail (pr. Ka trail) Kinard
Qatrail, Quetrail, Catrail, Cetrale (all pr. Ka trail)

Qesean (pr. Key shawn) & Qusean (pr. Q shawn) (inspired by twins)
Qeshaun, Qeesaun, Qeshaan
Qusaun, QShaun, Qshawn, Qsean, Qsaun

Qesaan (pr. Key sun) (inspired by best friend, Ebony's son's first name Kiesun)
Qesun, Kesun, Keisun, Qeson

Qavan (pr. Ka vaughn)

Qavah (inspired by Lamentation 3:25-26 means wait, pr. Kah vah)

Qi'Raf (pr. Ke raaf) & Qi'Nom (pr. Ke nom) (inspired by twins,

contributed by Hakim, 6/22/11)

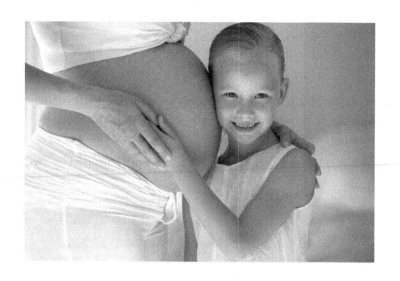

INSPIRED BY SCRIPTURE
GALATIANS 6:7-9

R—You shall *reap* a harvest of blessing.

Renzi & Renzo (inspired by twins)

Rienne

Ryan

Rielle

Renaa (pr. Ren ay)

Raynell, Rainelle

Rameesha, Ramisha

Rambert or Ramberto

Raville (inspired by Rayna & Deville) (pr. Ray vill)
  Raiville, Revile, Rayvil, Reivill

Rayna

Reannie

Rashon, Rashun, Rashaan

River

Rinnah (pr. Ree nah) Serene inspired by scripture Psalms 30:5, means joy, & Proverbs 11:10 means singing and jubilation, inspired by first & middle names

Rahim (pr. Ra heem) & Rakim (pr. Ra keem), (inspired by twins)

Radimir

Ranger

Raiden

Rance

Ralston

Rabaan (means glory of god in African, Hawaiian, and Hindu)

Raj (means king in Hebrew)

Rashid (means wise adviser in Swahili)

Raylan

Rishi (means sega of gods in Hindu)

Romero

Rossif

Raquan

Rinnah & Hannir (inspired by girl & boy twins names, spelled reciprocally)

Releacia, Releesia, Releasia, Releaseah (all pr. the same) inspired by "Released", song by Bill Winston, contributed 1/10/14

Riguel & Miguel (inspired by girl & boy twins, other pr. are Regelle, Reguel, or Raguel)

Retxed Melicio (inspired by first & middle name, from Dexter's name spelled backwards)

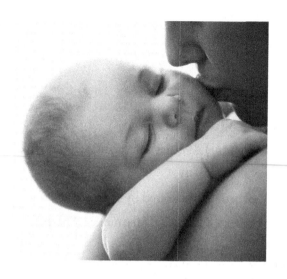

INSPIRED BY SONG BY DONNIE MCCLURKIN

S—After you've done all you can, you just *stand*.

Sharlesa

Shanice, Shanique, & Shandice (inspired by triplets)

Szemari (s or z can be silent)

Shalenda & Shaelinda (inspired by twins)

Stephani, Stephanie

Shianne & Shienna (inspired by twins)

Shariane & Sharianna (inspired by twins)

Shemiya & Shemilah (inspired by twins)

Syani, Tsyani (t is silent) (both pr. see on knee)

Sianne & Sianney (pr. sy annie) (inspired by twins)

Shemina & Shellina (inspired by twins)

Shaelyn

Semari & Sacani (inspired by twins)

Shaeza

Shandre

Secara & Zeckara (inspired by twins)

Shiayne (pr. Shi anne) & Shiayse (pr. Shi ace) (inspired by twins)

Shercanna

Sharnessa & Sharneissa (inspired by twins)

Sharneica, Sharneka, Charneka, Sharniquea, Sharneieqa, Sharnieqa (all pr. the same)

Serubi (inspired by a local street name) Naomi (inspired by first and middle name)

Shiheen

Shimeg, Shimeq, Shahmeg (all pr. the same)

Sharna & Charnay (inspired by twins)
     Charna, Sharneh, Charneh
     Sharnei, Charnei, Charneiy, Sharney

Semyia

Synonee

Senaa, Saneigh

Shakuena (pr. Sha queen ah)

Shallel & Shayelle (inspired by twins)

Starrah

Sebastian

Sylver

Sidney & Syndnea (inspired by twins)

Seaven (pr. 7 or Save en) & Savaan (pr. Sa Vaughn) (inspired by twins)

Sailur, Saylur, Sayler (all pr. the same)

Sajaica, Sajayca

Semaj (inspired by James spelled backwards)

Sanita & Saieda (pr. Si ee da) (inspired by twins)
    Saiida, Sieeda, Sieeta

Semar Kindia (inspired by first & middle name)

Sitrease, Citrice, Sitrice, Sitreace (all pr. the same)

Sorrell

Sky & Shy (inspired by twins)

Shaaz, Shazz, Shaz (8/31/09)

Stream (contributed 8/31/09)

Shadose (contributed 8/31/09)

Shatheed (contributed 9/22/10)

Satori, Sacori, & Saroti (inspired by triplets 1/7/2011)

Samoht (pr. Sa'moth, inspired by Hakim 6/22/11, Thomas spelled backwards)

Siuol (pr. Si ool, inspired by Hakim 6/22/11, Louis spelled backwards)

Samuol (pr. Sa mool, inspired by Hakim 6/22/11) & Samuel

Sivarj Amik & Siraj Ameki, inspired by twins, 7/13/11)

Shazar & Shaeza (contributed 8/20/12, inspired by twins)

Samoj (inspired by Joe & Thomas)

Shakuena (pr. Sha queen ah)

Shallel & Shayelle (inspired by twins)

Sethaniel (contributed 9/8/12)

Sejal

Seleathia & Seleaviya (inspired by twins)

Sadella & Sabella (inspired by twins, 1/3/14)

Sadorian & Sadore (inspired by boy & girl twins, 5/12/14)

Sabria

Simas & Sirias (pr. Serious) inspired by twins, 11/22/13

Shystelle & Shyster (inspired by girl & boy twins)

Sagirah (inspired by Almasi's sister's name, I met Almasi at Dr. Feldman's pediatric dental office, also inspired by Nadirah's name – I met Nadirah at COH church)

INSPIRED BY SCRIPTURE
PROVERS 3:5

T—*Trust* in the Lord with all thine heart.

Tiavanni & Teshanni (inspired by twins)

Tynerra Shanei & Tyana Chardei (both inspired by twins' first and middle names)

Trenton

Temarcus

Temari & Temarreah (inspired by twins, boy & girl)

Tanica

Taralyn & Taryn (inspired by twins, girl & boy)

Tiffani

Tarian & Tarianna (inspired by twins, boy & girl)
    Taryanna, Tyreanna

Tanique or Tineeq Jewel-Mae (inspired by first & middle)

Tameyah & Temiyla (inspired by twins)
    Temiila

Tyani, Teyani

Torren, Tyree, Toriey (inspired by triplets)

Tameryn & Tamerlyn (inspired by twins)

Taamerla & Taamerah (inspired by twins)
    Tamerlah
    Taamerha, Tamerrah

Trevon

Tychius & Tyria (inspired by twins, boy & girl)

Tameisa, Tamisa

Taishayla (pr. Ty shay lah) & Taiaja (pr. Ty asia) (inspired by twins)
    Tyshaila
    Tyasiha

Taj (pr. Tay-j) & Toj (T-haj) (inspired by twins)

Taren, Turen, Tyrin (inspired by triplets)
    Taran, Tyran, Tiren, Tyraan, Tyrun, Tyren

Tarene (pr. Tare ren knee) & Taranie (pr. Te rain knee) (inspired by twins)
    Tareneey, Tarenee, Tarenie
    Tarinee, Terinee, Terranie

Tyrian, Tyrien

Terianne, Theriann

Tyiland

Teeaja, TeAsia, TeaAja (all pr. the same) & Thaisha (pr. Ty asia) (inspired by twins)
    Tiescha, Tyescha

Traniqua (inspired by Tamayne & Arnekua)

Traneeq (inspired by Trameel & Monique)

Trimeeka & Trameesa (inspired by twins)
    Tremiqa
    Tremisa

Tromeka (inspired by Troy & Tamika)

Tavius, Taveus, Tavias (all pr. the same)

Tyairah (pr. Ty air a) & Taier (pr. Ty air)

Tyeirra, Thaiera

Taqueena

Tai, Tyai, Thiy, Tye (all pr. the same)

Taiyschka, Thaiscka, Taiyscka, Taishca (pr. Tye sha ka)

Teric, Terrick, Teriic, Terick (all pr. the same)

Travius, Traevius

Treainna & Treneice (inspired by twins)

Theangelo

Terranse, Terrance, Tarence (2007, all pr. the same)

Taures Turrel (inspired by first & middle name)

Teci, Tecee (pr. T C)

Taneya, Taneeya, Teiya, Teniiya (all pr. the same)

Tearia, Teeairea, Teairea (all pr. Tee air e ah)

Tashinee, Tashinaa, Tashenaa (all pr. Ta shin a)

Tang'kineka

Terris Zhundre (inspired by first & middle)

Taige, Teige

TaeVins & TaeRins (contributed 12/30/09)

Trinicee, Trinetcee (inspired by Trinity)

Tynera Ma'Vet & Tyren Lumas (inspired by twins by Hakim, 6/20/11)

Teiya (pr. T I ya, contributed 10/6/12)

Terianne, Theriann

Tanesia, Tenesia (contributed 6/20/11)

Tessh'kim (pr. Ta she kim, 6/2/11)

Taelene & Tawlene (contributed by Hakim, 6/22/11)

    Talene, Thalene & Taulene, Tolene

Thuwen & Thunson or Thussen (6/22/11)

Tacia (pr. Ta c ah, 6/22/11, Hakim)

Tatem & Tandem (inspired by twins 7/29/11)

Teladrin Chapelle (first & middle name)

Tielle (pr. T L, contributed 9/29/12)

Tawago (contributed 1998)

Tynera Ma'Vet & Tyren Lumas (inspired by twins by Hakim, 6/20/11)

Teiya (pr. T I ya, contributed 10/6/12)

Tsrida (pr. Sree ida – the t is silent) Adrist (inspired by first & middle name, reciprocal spellings,

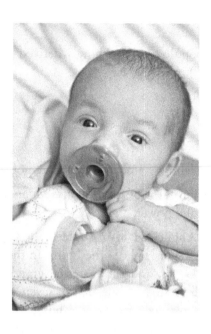

INSPIRED BY SCRIPTURE
PROVERS 8:8-9

U—God's words are plain to him
who *understands.*

Ungenay (pr. un gen nay, the way it looks, inspired by co-worker Angela)

Ungenlaa (pr. un gen lay)

Uriah (Hebrew name means Flame of Jehovah or my Light is Jehovah, inspired by Lareina Rule, author of Name Your Baby, 1986)

Uritza (pr. U ree za or U rit za) (contributed by Ebony, 7/24/09)

Ukiah & Uriyah (inspired by twins, contributed 10/6/12)

Udell

Udayan

Umar (means "populous, flourishing", derived from Arabic عمر ('umr) "life")

Ulik, Ulique (pr. U leek)

Uriella

Ulani

Udiel (לְאִ.יד.אוּ): Hebrew name meaning "torch of the Lord."

Ulrik: Scandinavian form of Old High German Ulrich, meaning "prosperity and power."

Uriel (לְ.אִ.יר.אוּ): Anglicized form of Hebrew Uwriyel, meaning "flame of God" or "light of the Lord." In the bible, this is the name of a Levite, and the maternal grandfather of Abijah. It is also the name of one of the seven archangels whose names were removed from the Church's list of recognized angels in 145 A.D. He was said to have been one of the angels stationed at God's throne. He was considered the wisest of the archangels because his light was not merely of the physical kind, but rather the ultra-spiritual kind, making him highly intellectually illuminated. Some think Uriel was the angel who warned Noah of the coming flood, and helped the prophet Ezra interpret a prediction concerning the coming Messiah. He is also said to be the angel of divine magic, alchemy, writing, earthquakes, floods, and other kinds of cataclysms. (http://www.20000-names.com/male_u_names.htm)

Uziel Variant spelling of English

Uzziel, meaning "God is my strength."

INSPIRED BY SCRIPTURES
MATTHEW, MARK, LUKE, JOHN

V—*Verily* I say unto you.

Vanessa Olivia (inspired by first & middle name)

Velisa & Venisa (inspired by twins)

    Veleisa

    Veneisa

Vonshenay

Verrill (contributed 10/6/12)

Vander

Varick

Vachel

Vanya

Vali

Verina

Valonia

Vasuda (means "granting wealth" in India)

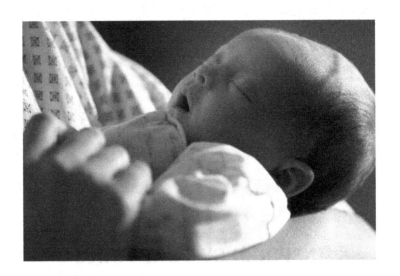

INSPIRED BY SCRIPTURES
PSALMS 27: 8-14, 37: 4

W—*Wait* on the Lord and he shall give you the desires of your heart.

Worrell (Old English name means dweller at the true man's manor, inspired by Lareina Rule, author of Name Your Baby, 1986)

Wren (means chief or ruler, inspired by Lareina Rule, author of Name Your Baby, 1986)

Winter Rose (inspired by my son's friend's name in daycare)

Wardell (contributed 10/6/12)

Wahib

Waltrina

Whistar & Whynstell (inspired by twins)

Wanetta

Wysandra

Wakana

Washeeti

Wystan

Wakaun

Walida

Walston & Winston (inspired by twins)

INSPIRED BY WORDS OF ENCOURAGEMENT

X—*Express* yourself.

Xamorius Katavian (inspired & contributed by Cousin Victoria, 2008)

Xzavion (contributed by Ebony, 2008)

Xoana (contributed 10/6/12)

Xabi

Xylia

Xanthe

Xannon

INSPIRED BY SCRIPTURE
PSALMS 119:11

Y—*Your* word have I hidden in my heart that I might sin against thee.

Yorec (inspired by Corey with interchangeable letters, pr. your ray, with c being silent)

Yorima, Yurima, Yurema (all pr. the same, inspired by Yuri & Sharema)

Yachal (inspired by Micah 7:7, means wait)

Yandell (inspired by Suelain May, author of Names to Grow On, 2007)

Ynohtna (pr. yah ten a) (inspired by Anthony spelled backwards, contributed by friend Shawanna's daughter's name)

Yashar (inspired by scripture Proverbs 3:6, means to be straight, upright, pleasing, good)

Yanira (contributed by Ebony, 9/17/10)

Yulissa (contributed by Ebony, 9/17/10)

Yaritza (contributed by Ebony, 9/17/10)

Yoj (inspired by Joy spelled backwards, 6/25/11)

Yamil Limay (pr. Lee may) (inspired by first & middle name, reciprocal spellings, Yamil in Spanish means – You are mine)

Yuri Iruy (inspired by first & middle names, spelled reciprocally)

Yakima Amikay (inspired by first & middle names, spelled reciprocally)

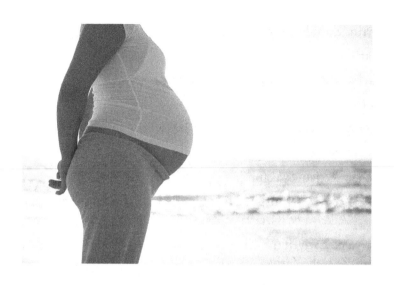

INSPIRED BY SCRIPTURE
ROMANS 10:2

Z—Have a *zeal* for God.

Zahavia Dellaney & Zharia Melanie (inspired by both first & middle name and twins)
>Dellaney is inspired by Dexter & Melanie or Della & Anthony.

Zander, Zandia, Zandrea (inspired by triplets)

Zavier

Zakeri & Zaterri (inspired by twins)

Zephani

Zachery (pr. Za care ee)

Zared, Zered (inspired by Numbers 21:2, 8/31/09)

Zelina, Zeninah, & Zaleema (inspired by triplets)

Zyri

Zorrin, Zorrah, Zorriah (inspired by triplets)

Zhari

Zikeba & Zekiva (inspired by twins)

Zori

Zeiel (pr. Zi elle) & Zeal (inspired by twins)

Zakesia & Zakisa (inspired by twins)

Zacheus & Jaqueyas (pr. Jack que us) (inspired by twins)

Zakeia & Kizeya (inspired by twins, letters used interchangeably)
    Zakeiya & Kizeeya or Zakeeia & Kazeiya

Zuriya & Zariyeh (pr. Zhar ee a) (inspired by twins)
    Zaryeh, Zariye

Zuri (means beautiful in Swahili)

Zyair, Zyare

Zyree, Zahre

Zrianna, Zreanna

Zetauni, Zsatauni, Zetanni (all pr. the same)

Ziana & Zion (inspired by twins)
    Zian, Zyane, Zyion, Ziyon

Zarrius Zaquey, Zacheus Zachii, & Zerrana Zannei
(all inspired by first & middle names, triplets)
    Zacchaeus means pure, Zaccai means pure, inspired by
    Ezra 2:9,
    Nehemiah 7:14, Luke 19:1-10, 12-27 from Easton Bible
    Dictionary
    Zaccai is same pr. as Zachii, also Zackaa, Zachaay, or
    Zachaey (all pr. the same)
    (all three first names are 7 letters and all three middle names
    are 6 letters)

Zamerr & Zamerio (inspired by twins)

Zundreia, Zundriea, Zundreay, Zundriay, Zundriey (all pr. zun
dray ah)

Zabriston Jabronte (inspired by Cousin)

Zacain, Zacaan (means ancient, something that grows with age, inspired by Psalms 119:100)

Zacharias & Zacchaeus (inspired by twins)

Zhan (contributed 7/30/09) & Zannah (contributed by church friend Rhonda's daughter's name, other pr. Zahnna or Zaana

Ziyah, Zahya, Zayah (contributed 9/2/10)

Zohar

Zaqan or Zaqon (pr. Za con)

Zonal (pr. Zo nalle)

Zoan & Ziyon (inspired by twins)

Zellanie

Zeann (pr. Z ann)

Zico (contributed 12/30/09)

Zaviere

Zaquila (inspired by student Jaquila)

Zara (inspired by scripture Hosea 10:12, means to sow or plant seeds in order to increase returns)

Zichri (inspired by 1 Chronicles 26:25, 6/26/11)

Zanoel Jarel & Zanoah Asarel (inspired by twins, contributed 1/15/14, inspired by scripture I Chronicles 4:16-18)

Zyari & Azaria (inspired by twins)

Zyarmi & Zynavi (inspired by twins)

Zenarmi & Zenovie (inspired by twins)

Printed in the United States
By Bookmasters